A True Survivor's Journey To Real Life

Pursuing Adventure & Overcoming
Tragedy To Find Real Life

By Paul Snyder

A True Survivor's Journey To Real Life

Pursuing Adventure & Overcoming

Tragedy To Find Real Life

Published & Printed In The United States Of America

Dedication To Jerry, Rudy & Servant Leaders

No project is a success without hard work, inspiration, and encouragement from many people. This book is no exception. I dedicate this endeavor to Jerry whose legacy is explained in chapter ten. His strong character and tenacity live on in my life's major decisions. Jerry, thank you for all you did for me.

It is also dedicated to my adopted family's "Rudy." Brother, I did not have the honor to know you personally, however, love and respect your family. I've learned you were larger than life! Jerry and Rudy loved from deep places, places most never find. They lived out a secret few learn: How you live and serve matters.

Below are servant leaders sacrificially invested in and opening major doors for my life: SSgt. Van Horn, U.S. Ambassador William D. Clarke, GySgt. Riveria, SSgt Wilshire (RIP), Sgt. Martin, Sgt. Vanloon (RIP), Sgt. Major Page., Colonel M. You wisely guided my Marine Corps steps.

A SOUTHCOM Chief Master Sergeant, Scott, Jeff, Colonel M, Greg, Mark, Brad, Bill, Michael P, Jean, Kraig, and Bob (and dozens more). You guided my security and risk management global service (1998 - 2018) providing mentorship, training, perspectives, answering questions, opening great doors.

"DT" Gary, Deputy J, Les, Big "Mac," Colonel J, "Donny," Jesse, "Funny Man" Chris, Director Babb, Stefan, Jason, Seth, Joni, AZ DPS and Greater Phoenix Agencies Command Staff, PHX PD senior officers, ATAP-AZ Board, and Class 74 Command Staff and Trainers. I owe my success on Arizona's streets to your modeling law enforcement excellence. I'll continue applying those lessons the next two decades.

Finally, I thank God, my incredible family, Colonel M, Brad, and Phoenix adopted "lifers" Sam, Mia, Santi, Josi and your families who have shared your lives. I respect, love, and appreciate you! I am paying it forward!

Paul

YOU WILL FIND YOUR JOY IN THE LORD AND RIDE IN TRIUMPH ON THE HEIGHTS OF THE LAND.
- ISAIAH 58:14

Adopted Brother Rudy (EOW: March 2017)

VFW, Vice Commander, Marine, Desert Storm Veteran

Rest in Peace Brother I Will Help Care For Your Family

Table of Contents

A True Survivor's Journey To Real Life

Personal Note From Author

Dear Reader,

Thank you for investing time to read "an eagle's flight" over my global adventures, challenges, adversities, and triumphs. I hope you're inspired to live more courageously and on purpose.

Life is beautiful, tough, complicated, and incredible. It WILL test our mettle, resolve, and character. It will battle to steal your heart, integrity, and perspective. We never know what is down the road. However, WE CAN be well prepared with unstoppable character.

I've had the privilege to serve around the globe, observing the best and worst of humanity. I've experienced joy, friendship, and success. I've journeyed through tragedies, overcome "impossible" obstacles, and walked through the valley of the shadow of death.

By sharing part of my story, I pray you'll chose to be more intentional about YOUR life. I pray this story ignites a growing flame to share your unique story with those with whom you have influence and find special ways to serve others!

What will they say at your memorial service? Will you have lived out your purpose? Will you have invested in others? Will you stay your course once you've found your purpose?

Will you refuse to allow circumstances, naysayers, setbacks, rejections, tragedies, even life-threatening challenges to define the impact your life?

Considering my family tree, I may have another forty plus years however no one gets guarantees. Come join me in challenging your faith, finding service to others, refusing mediocrity, and finishing your race strong.

Know Your Direction. Know Your Why.

Stay Your Course. *Paul*

Chapter One

The Early Years. The Journey Begins

There are no great people in this world, only great challenges which ordinary people rise to meet." Fleet Admiral W. F. Halsey, Jr.

Walker, Iowa. A borough of barely six hundred people. Farm support, blue collar workers, a hardware store, granary, even a dairy queen. Every town needs a great dairy queen!

The favorite spot for the town's people on hot summer evenings. The taste of hot fudge sundaes, the cold thrill of vanilla ice cream covered in caramel for the kids. A town so small we had no middle or high school.

Life was simple, uncomplicated. Midwest values, very hard work, integrity, and human decency were common. Values driven by one's word to perform as promised. Many neighbors had backyard gardens raising their vegetables, canning them for the cold months to come.

That snow-covered January of 1965, I breathed my first breath at St. Luke's being escorted to the hospital by a county deputy sheriff. Shortly after that frozen midnight, my father was attempting to preempt my arrival by being at the hospital first. After realizing my arrival was imminent, the deputy decided not to ticket my father, leaving us far behind "clearing" the road ahead, running code 3 (lights and siren) that frigid day in central Iowa.

Little did my parents know that night type arrival foreshadowed future years working with and alongside state, federal, and diplomatic law enforcement around our globe.

My early years were filled with imagination, adventures, hard work and wonderful memories. Building forts in the dense woods alongside the train tracks. Designing snowmen in our freezing winters, sweating in our family garden, and racing home after Sunday evening church to watch Sanford & Son, followed by popcorn, sodas, and treats Mom created in her Sunday night kitchen.

Games, jokes, and warm memories from early years linger as I can see that kitchen. It was the center of our home. Where it all happened.

On weeknights, our home was filled with the sounds of Emergency, The Brady Bunch, Partridge Family, and Little House On The Prairie. The values of personal responsibility and treating others with respect and integrity were engrained in all six of us. There were no excuses for not resolving differences and conflicts.

Each child in our family learned sweat equity having their own rows of responsibility in a huge family garden. The working end of a shovel, rototiller, hoe, picking weeds, and ensuring every row produced tons of vegetables kept our table filled with delicious food through the cold winters until early summer.

These family work sessions were filled with water breaks, delicious picnic meals, lots of laughter, bantering amongst us kids, followed by more sweat to finish the tasks at hand.

One of my fondest memories was our family dressing up in 1800's hand-designed outfits, and my father/s pitch black beard, all dressed in black, with stove top hat, looking quite like Abe Lincoln. We then traveled to a Cedar Rapids ball park for an 1800 era custom competition.

I remember shopping in Walkers' hardware store, riding bikes all over, and trips to a friend's farm where we learned to care for, feed, and ride the horses by the age of eight.

Long rides along river trails and learning farm values where everyone pulled their weight.

I learned to respect these large animals' powerful hoofs after the first time under their body weight. They remain the most magnificent of all animals to this day. Years later, I would own a magnificent Arabian Stallion in Cairo named Eagle.

By ten years of age, I had well-toned muscles, a lean frame, and dark tan from hard work in our garden and time on the farm. I was learning the importance of physical fitness to success in life.

These fitness foundations would serve me well later in the Marines, law enforcement, and running half marathons and Tough Mudder competitive events.

Fitness remains a core value today, eventually leading me to finding the deeper Real Life this book is all about. I share how that process becoming life changing in Chapter Ten.

Chapter Two

The Teenage Years

"Have a plan. Work your plan."
Life Mentor Gordon Decker

The years before college were filled with moving to Michigan, landing my first job as a paper carrier and working full time on a massive hog farm prior to college.

I had a bright green bike complete with steel, side baskets and a route of up to 60 clients over a 5-mile route. Rain or shine, the paper must be delivered.

I dreaded Sundays papers! They had extra thick ad inserts and were very heavy. I had both steel baskets stuffed to overflowing, wearing a canvas bag over my shoulder to carry the remainder. It wasn't until half through the route, the weight became comfortable.

This daily work continued toning my body for the Babe Ruth baseball and long days to come on the farm before college. The "pain" was a blessing in the disguise of "preparation."

It was on this massive hog farm, I learned the value of making a plan and following that plan. A friend hired me into their family operation by fifteen.

My buddy's family annually raised approximately 10,000 - 15,000 pigs each year. We worked hard through rain, snow, shine on their family farms in Cass County Michigan.

From early morning chores to late night feeding operations, from falling into dirty pen if you lost your balance, you learned self-awareness and life safety sprinting from "momma" sow (350+ lbs.) suddenly deciding you were in the wrong place at the wrong time!

Those years were filled with laughter, ribbing family members, and as the "city slicker" you first earned your respect amongst this hard-working family.

My lifer buddy Dale taught me to drive every kind of John Deere tractor, farm equipment, and operating machinery they had.

You had to be like a jack of all trades. You could be tasked with any dozen of daily projects and you had to know how to do with your eyes nearly closed.

Those years of big farm lunches, deep friendship, laughter, and exhaustion formed the foundation of an ever-growing work ethic I carry sacred today.

An outstanding work ethic. Just another key part of finding Real Life.

Chapter Three

College & Boot Camp: A New Direction

Seek and you will find. The Bible

I attended community colleges and universities in Indiana and Michigan majoring in pre-med and animal science studies.

My first near death experience occurred in a small Indiana town while attending college. I had borrowed a buddy's car making a store run. During my drive back, an intoxicated man ran a stop sign, crushing, and totaling the Volkswagen Beatle I was driving with his tank size 1970's

Buick Electra. Think elephant squashing a small bug. Score: Elephant one. Bug zero!

I remember the deafening, crushing noise, as this Electra tank t-boned the driver's door and my head smashed against the driver's window, shattering it. Lights out.

I came to finding paramedics working on me, then extricating me from Beetle , asking lots of questions I tried to answer, then they transported me to the emergency room minutes away.

All I knew was my head hurt! I had a
neck brace on. After treatment for hours, then
ER observation, I was released late that evening
to my roommate's care (bed rest) the next few
days. Although sandwiched in this bug's front
seat, I survived with no long-term injuries.

Like a summer camp's encounter (at
nine!) with a baseball bat to my throat (accident
near batting box), and surviving, again, death
was cheated because it wasn't my time.

With no personal responsibility assessed
for these accidents, I knew early on, it simply
wasn't my time. I continued playing softball for

another decade, however, never again drove a Beetle.

I was gifted academically graduating top of my high school class. However, after only three years of college, my restlessness had grown for new adventure, to serve my Country, and see the world. This car accident only fueled my desire to travel and see the world while I still "had time."

After checking the different services, I settled on the Marines. The Few. The Proud. The Marines. If I was going to serve, I wanted one of the toughest boot camps. I sought out the rigors of a lifestyle that would significantly challenge me. I knew the Marines would push me to my limits, ensuring I was ready for whatever came after the Marines.

I did not tell my parents until after I enlisted, not knowing my family had only known Marines brought home from Vietnam in body bags. Unknowingly, I become the subject of thousands of hours of my Mother's faithful prayers as I went off to see the world, serve in dangerous roles, and make my way in the world.

In my early twenties, I believed I was invincible. In the Marines, on and off duty, I was always seeking out the next tougher adventure and challenge.

It would require two decades of deepening maturity, experiencing tragedies around the globe, to temper me as I still pursue great challenges, however reduce risks whenever possible, and enjoy keeping people safer wherever I can.

Little did I know this enlistment decision would change my life's projectory leading to future career roles, global endeavors and relationships nurtured since 1989.

Looking back, it changed my life, forging major portions of my life foundation, character, work life, and lifetime of mutually beneficial relationships.

In 1989, I shipped to boot camp in San Diego, California. Every Marine remembers "that" unforgettable bus ride and yellow foot prints that forever change your life!

What a wake-up call! Immediately, my life experience, presence, and size set me apart for special attention. I was informed I would be pushed harder. I would be assigned leadership roles serving our Senior Drill Instructor and given extra exercises my first thirty days.

Just like clockwork, it all happened as promised! Our drill instructors always followed through. Dependability was drilled in our minds, bodies and souls from Day 1. They ensured we came to live, breath, and act Semper Fidelis (Latin for Always Faithful).

At six two, two hundred thirty pounds, the long runs, thousands of pushups and sit-ups, eight count body builders, obstacle courses, and squad bay exercises (exercises I had never heard of!) quickly reduced me to an ultra-lean two hundred sixteen pounds. Having endured grueling wrestling and soccer workouts, prior to the Marines, the harder they pushed, the more I put my head down and excelled.

Sergeant Dove and Yarborough pushed me beyond my (known) limits ensuring I was mentally and physically tough enough for the next nine years in the Marines. I will never forget their faces or great examples they set for me. Thank you Gentlemen!

Graduation came quickly in June 1989. Months had flown by. While a blur, much was taught, learned, and practiced hundreds of times in crucibles of pain, pain, and more pain. Many times, we heard, Pain is Weakness Leaving the Body. It was true. I was tougher, stronger than ever before in my life at graduation.

My cousin traveled from Los Angeles for graduation. It was great to be reunited with him following the graduation parade, however, we had only minutes, after the ceremony, before returning to our barracks to receive our tickets home for 10 days leave.

Prior to attending Motor Transport school at Camp Pendleton, I traveled to Michigan to see my parents, friends, and relax a few days. My parents couldn't believe how lean I was. My Mom did her best to fatten me up before I returned to California for my specialty school ten days later.

By late June 1989, I was back in Del Mar, California for Motor Transport Operator School. That six-week school raced by, and I became a gym rat from Day 1. I began extreme workouts, sometimes doing hundreds of sit-ups each evening, running off duty, and pushing myself to peak levels of fitness.

My body fat percentage fell below seven percent while I ate whatever I wanted. I burned it off every night in the gym or running on the shores of the Pacific.

I loved running on the Pacific's beaches at Del Mar. The ocean had a call all its own. I would spend hundreds of hours in the water (off duty) surviving my third, near-death experience in Pacific waters off South America a few years later.

Before Motor Transport School graduation, I requested overseas assignment, as during formations we watched, nearby, as new US Navy corpsmen trained to head to the Fleet

Marine Force. Little did I know my first unit would be a Navy Battalion in Okinawa.

Chapter Four

Marines 1989 - 1993 (Part 1)

Ask not what your Country can do for you. Ask what you can do for your Country. President John F. Kennedy

I flew through Alaska enroute the Far East. I was assigned to Third Marine Forces Service Support Group (3rd FSSG), Camp Hansen, Okinawa. Excitement was in my veins. I was finally traveling to see the world and serve my Country.

From the time I hit the ground, I remained a gym rat, hitting the old squad bay styled gym five days a week, doing ruck sack runs, completing long runs outside Camp Hansen, in addition to the required three times weekly unit exercises.

I loved the challenge of pushing myself to the next level and never finished a workout until I was drenched in sweat.

During this assignment, I met the one man who shaped my Marine career, post Marine career, and life now working in and around the first responder communities.

Staff Sergeant Van Horn, while quiet, was quite imposing, standing a rock solid 205 lbs. at six foot 3 inches. Built like a Mac truck, SSgt. Van Horn was a body builder having placed well in many competitions.

He watched me through my first four months of working for him in Okinawa. He ensured I was detailed to Team Spirit 1990 (South Korea) and provided extraordinary opportunities to serve senior leadership and numerous command staff there.

In Korea, I was assigned to work with the Marine Military Police and Corpsman on shore patrol. Those nights on the town, working, were never dull. There was always some Sailor or Marine getting themselves in serious trouble out on liberty.

We had a homemade gym set up on our ocean side base so we could get our workouts in several times a week between long duty shifts. Life was great, with exciting, new challenges every day which we were expected to find solutions to.

Sadly, it was in South Korea, I lost my first Marine brother. I had the distinct honor to personally assist in his transport to Taegu where we met his Sergeant Major before he was flown to the United States and to his family for burial.

There were always reminders like this, in trainings or deployments, that our career could be unforgiving, so the better prepared, the better chances you would survive. Or as we would said: "always be prepared and you will survive if it is not your time."

Returning from Team Spirit, SSgt Van Horn immediately recommended me for special duty with the U.S. State Department's Marine Security Guard program (MSG). It was considered a special assignment, like being a

Drill Instructor or Recruiter. If you excelled in any of these three specialties, it was extra helpful to your future career.

At the time, the washout rate for MSG School was approximately 40% of those arriving in Quantico to start the demanding six-week school. Should you fail, it was a mark you did NOT want on the pages of your military records. Those who graduated served U.S. Embassies, Consulates or specialty support assignments supporting the MSG mission for the State Department.

Regardless of rank, the pressure during this school was constant and unending. Fifteen plus hour days were common place. The pace was demanding. Our days started pre-dawn always lasting late into the night. Even weekly Marine Corps fitness requirements (three-unit exercise times weekly) were completed on our "off duty" time each week.

There were no excuses. Put out or go home to the Fleet. There was no room for individuals or selfishness. MSG units world-wide demanded critical thinking, highly fit, exceptional professionals, able to handle any challenge.

Failure "at post" could mean an international incident, security breaches, harm to persons and property when the job didn't get done. International news had been made the recent years in Russia with Sergeant Lonetree and the Marine detachment in Lima, Peru being relieved for cause.

All you had to say was "I'm done." Many in my MSG class quit the first few days after working for months to arrive at Quantico for this specialty school. I put my head down doing whatever was required each day, ensuring I, and my entire squad were prepared for the next day.

By working hard with my squad, most of us survived knowing the sacrifices were worth it.

Many nights, I used the treadmill, pumped iron in the old basement gym, then ironed my "cammies" late into the night working hard to keep my eyes open, not severely burning my hands with the old steam machines afterwards. Constant room, uniform, and locker inspections were common place.

The demands to graduate as Ambassadors in Blue was high. You could be standing a lonely post, for hours, then meeting foreign Ambassadors, attending Diplomatic Receptions, or meeting the President or others traveling overseas on Diplomatic Missions. You never knew. You had to bring your A game every day.

MSG Graduation! Another blur of days and weeks running together. We had made it! I was assigned to US Embassy Cairo, Egypt during Desert Storm and Desert Shield and later to US Embassy Lima, Peru.

Within two days, five of us were on the ground in Cairo supporting President Bush and Barbara's visit to the middle east. It was an incredible privilege to work closely with the U.S. Secret Service for the first of many times across my career. We had the privilege of meeting General (Stormin') Norman and many senior Washington, D. C. leadership during the "first" Gulf War.

I had the privilege to visit the U.S.S. America steaming home from the Gulf. The Assistant Air Boss and Command Staff gave us a full tour as we met the hard-working deck crews, tail hook operators, corpsmen, Marines, Pilots, and crew teams on the carrier.

We took the Marine Security Detachment members specialty items from Cairo's Khan Al

Khalili as we knew their long hours in the Gulf had been taxing and they would appreciate it.

Half way through my Cairo tour, I was selected as a world-wide finalist and meritorious promotion candidate.

During this tour, I had the privilege to work closely with Diplomatic Security Service Agents (DSS) serving U.S. Secretary of State James A. Baker in both Cairo and Damascus. I found Secretary Baker to be warm and genuinely approachable. His reputation as a first-class, diplomatic statesman was exactly how I experienced him.

The Secretary set aside time to talk directly with me while on duty outside his personal suite late one night.

I had the honor of working with the True Professionals of the U.S. Secret Service and Diplomatic Security Service on dozens of occasions, during training, and in several countries.

These men and women are the finest our Nation has, deserving our gratitude for lives of extreme sacrifice made every day. Their helpfulness, training expertise, and willingness to invest in MSG's was something we always appreciated during training cycles and operations. It was this first exposure to federal and diplomatic law enforcement that would lead later to service in sworn law enforcement nearly two decades later.

These professionals lit a fire in my soul that service to something greater than self was noble, right, and reasonable.

As an MSG, no matter where assigned, I found a place to run, pump iron, or hit the gym. Fitness was now a lifestyle! I didn't feel right if I missed a day (or two) due to operational commitments. I found my workouts were my sanctuary. They became my place to process life, make key decisions, to maintain clarity and focus for life. This fitness lifestyle later led to half marathons and Tough Mudder(s) as I sought new fitness challenges in my post Marine years.

Sadly, I lost my second and third Marine Brothers from Cairo. A Staff NCO and my own Sergeant were to pass. One in combat and one years later in the United States. I honor them both here.

Both men poured into my life and character in Cairo. Both believed in me and pushed me hard ensuring I reached my full potential.   Rest in Peace My Brothers.   We have the watch from here SSgt Wilshire. Yes, it's now time "to make the pancakes" in Heaven, Sgt. Van Loon.

In Cairo, I enjoyed playing my second year of international rugby. We played the Black and Whites, the British Royal Navy, the Fijians, Aussies, and many international teams. We only lost to the rugged Fijians that year – they were built like tree trunks and ran like gazelles!

Several of us purchased Arabian stallions, riding our prized horses near the Pyramids. On longer days off, we took day trip excursions with our dates and friends.

My Arabian, Eagle, was a mixture of grey, splashed with whites throughout his mane and across his face and body. Only his stable master, a British expat and I were allowed to ride him. He was incredibly strong, I rarely rode him "full out" because he was next to impossible to rein back in. There were always a few Marines in Cairo knowing the finer art of horsemanship and who were great to ride with in Cairo.

From Cairo, my Commanding Officer granted me my first duty station request. In

1992, I chose Lima, Peru which was one of the most dangerous MSG posts world-wide. I left Cairo with a record book jammed full of team driven achievements my squad Sergeant had led our team towards to help our Detachment excel.

I had found the life of dedication, service, and adventure I had always sought. I would pursue dozens of new global adventures off duty too, always serving local orphanages, making school character presentations, serving community centers, and managing large landscape overhaul projects until 2012 until unthinkable tragedies entered my life.

It would be the life lessons learned from chosen hardships (1990 - 2011), the resilient character learned from leadership mentors, and always serving others that would help me overcome those tragedies.

Those traits, along with strong faith, lifer friends, and loving family would help me overcome the tragedies to come.

Chapter Five

Marines 1989 - 1993 (Part 2)

What has violence ever accomplished? What has it ever created? No martyr's cause has ever been stilled by an assassin's bullet. No wrongs have ever been righted by riots and civil disorders…the uncontrollable mob is only the voice of madness, not the voice of the people. Robert Kennedy

Lima, Peru. March 1992. Violence. Bombings. Death. Political unrest. Ten days before I landed in Lima, President Fujimori declared martial law, absolving the Peruvian Congress and closing its Supreme Courts.

58

Military tanks and troops were stationed in front of the Supreme Court and check points were everywhere. Our Embassy was shelled by rockets during my time there. Bombings were every day occurrences. At times, you were just down the street, or on duty, when the ground shook under you.

The downtown shopping venue Miraflores had one car bomb detonated during day light hours taking lives and leaving many tons of debris. This car bombing shaved off the entire side of a high-rise apartment and store building and looked like a war zone.

Sendero Luminoso (The Shining Path) was fighting against the Peruvian government for control, seeking to disable the political, monetary, and markets of the capital of Lima.

Our MSG Lima detachment was highly trained. We were always ready responding to many incidents during my tour.

I had the privilege to help train the detail of Peruvian special operators assigned by our host government to protect our Ambassador. These hard-working men put their hearts and souls into their training to ensure they were ready for anything. It was an honor to work with them!

In Lima, I was assigned the privilege of leading our Detachment's physical training program. From pre-dawn, ten-mile runs, to Jujutsu, to close quarters combat, U.S. Embassy emergency response training--we did it all. No two fitness regimens were the same. Our Detachment Commander was an avid long-distance runner and his leadership kept us highly prepared.

We remained ready for the unexpected.

Our Gunnery Sergeant told us we could count on one constant. Violence would come. Lima's violence always delivered during 1992 - 1993. Every week when we were on and off duty. By being exceptionally prepared, we could stay alive to serve our Country another day.

Together, this tightly bonded detachment achieved special recognitions and awards while ensuring the Lima Embassy, its team, and property remained safe 24/7. We our owe success to our Detachment Commander's great mentorship. Thank you Gunny!

While assigned to Lima, a couple MSG's and I took a day trip to relax at the Pacific Ocean and rejuvenate. It was an incredible day enjoying the surf, Pacific, and the balmy South American day!

A strong swimmer, having taken youth, Marine and summer swim qualifications courses, I had learned to respect the water and especially the Ocean. Having dived in the Pacific (Okinawa 1989 - 1991), I had come to respect the Pacific's beauty, strength, and sometimes, unforgiving nature. The water had always been my place to unwind and get away just like the gym.

As this afternoon wore on, I was suddenly swept into a fast-developing undertow that repeatedly pulled me under. For many heart pounding minutes, I fought for my life, desperately fighting to swim sideways, and out of this life-threatening tide to the jagged rocks nearby.

My scuba training days in Okinawa had taught me to avoid at all costs the Pacific riptides that can take your life. You must swim to the side of a rip tide (or undertow) -- never parallel or stay within the life taking tide. Otherwise you can die from total exhaustion (inside the tide) taking you out to sea against your will.

The undertow kept pulling me under time after time for what seemed like an eternity. I would fight back to the surface for the air I needed to stay alive. This went for several minutes, when finally, when I thought it was going to die, I finally broke free, swimming the final approximately fifty yards to the rocky side shoreline.

Like others experiencing near death experiences, I saw my life "flash" before my eyes. I held onto the jagged rocks exhausted, closing my eyes and thanking God for being alive.

I was so glad to be alive! There are few feelings like those experienced near death. I have never forgotten that day. I knew there was more to accomplish, love to give, community service to be involved with.

This was my third near brush with death. First at a summer camp, later in that Indiana car accident, and now thousands of miles away in the South American Pacific.

As we say in the Marines, it was NOT my time that day. There was clearly a Higher Power attending my path. It would be those same two

truths that would help me overcome severe
tragedy nearly two decades later.

Chapter Six

Marines (1994 - 1997)

Be faithful in small things because it is in
them that your strength lies.
Mother Teresa

In August 1993, I returned to the United States being honorably discharged the first time as a Sergeant. Within months, I was busy in my new civilian life. I was working full time for a non-profit group on their night shift, doubling as trained site security.

Shortly after, I activated my USMC Reserve option to serve as the Headquarters and Support (H & S) Platoon Sergeant with Charlie 1/24th a Marine infantry unit.

I ran the armory for this combat veteran unit recently returned from Desert Storm and Desert Shield. I coordinated armed convoy security to and from training deployments for heavy weapons and Command Support Gear and managed training qualifications for fellow H & S Platoon Marines.

We had a highly motivated group of Marines who put their all into training and every

task our Commanding Officer passed down.
From January 1993 - March 1995, I helped lead
this Platoon, until re-enlisting for a second active
duty tour with the Marines. I raised my right
hand a second time, in late March 1995, and the
Commanding Officer, Recruiting Command, re-
enlisted me back into active duty with orders to
Camp Lejeune.

I reported to Camp Lejeune, North
Carolina, for Heavy Equipment Operator School
with dozens of "retread" Marines, who like me,
had re-enlisted, bringing experienced, non-
commissioned officers back into the Corps to
cover short falls in several specialties. We

showed up with our Alphas, having rows of ribbons and badges on them. Most of us were high threat theatre or combat veterans.

The majority reporting for school were "boots" fresh out of boot camp. Needless to say, the Duty NCO's were trying to figure where these experienced, combat veteran NCO's were coming from.

Our Staff NCO's assigned us to run school formations, inspections, and most administrative functions, relieving them of direct day to day leadership responsibilities. School flew by and I received orders to Okinawa August 1995, shipping out immediately at graduation. I had the privilege of being The Distinguished Graduate from my class and was assigned to 3rd FSSG, 9th Engineer Support Battalion (ESB), Camp Hansen. The unit was located in the exact motor pool where years earlier I had worked for SSgt. Van Horne. It was like coming home.

At our arrival on "the Rock" all onboarding Marines were briefed by Base Legal Authorities at Camp Foster before being transported to our new units. While our planes flew to the Rock, the international story of a brave, little Okinawa girl, who had been terrorized, then assaulted by a drunk, off duty sailor and two Marines had made international headlines. The very thought made of us sick to our stomachs and we found out one of the dishonorable thugs had been assigned to 9th ESB.

The Camp Hansen base was on lock down, daily protests were occurring and off duty trips severely restricted for all Americans. I had volunteered directly outside the Camp Hansen base in 1989- 1990 and scuba dived with the Hansen Serviceman's Center Director and Base Chaplain. With this history, the Battalion Colonel drafted a Command Letter, with personal signature, directing I could go to the Serviceman's Center anytime I desired. I was thankful for his favor and trust!

It was a tremendous help that the current Director of the Center was a courageous, three-time purple heart winner. Ernie and Bobbie, who ran the center had both served in the Marine Corps and genuinely loved the Okinawan people, servicemen, and women.

Six months later, through my Chain of Command, I again approached my Colonel, with Ernie's backing, and then went to our Commanding General 3rd FSGG, seeking permission for 9th ESB's Heavy Equipment Platoon to overhaul the grounds and property of the Hansen Serviceman Center. Our hope was to re-build a little trust, hope and faith with those hurt by this little girl's tragedy.

The Command General approved project day turned out beautiful, and heavy equipment, dumpers, front end loaders, and excavators, did tremendous work turning the center into a professional looking facility.

Working with gracious volunteers, led by a senior Marine officer (Greg), the center building was sanded and re-painted giving the old building more years of service to the community.

As my second Okinawa tour ended, I received orders to Marine Corps Air Station (MCAS), Yuma, Arizona. Little did I know, a decade later I'd be recruited back to Arizona by a former White House Attorney General to help his team set up global security and risk management operations.

Duty in Yuma flew by, I continued pumping iron, running the base dirt trails, and hanging out off duty with a close buddies and "Doc" our favorite duty US Navy Corpsman.

We took many off-duty trips to San Diego, Jacumba and other close over the border, southwest cities to enjoy our time off.

Our unit CSSD-16 was a Marine Air Wing Support Group key component for bi-annual fighter pilots' desert operations support. Our teams provided field transport, wrecker, fuel, communications and resupply support to forward elements supporting the pilot operations.

This operation ran approximately two weeks, however, with pre and post operations required up to eight weeks of total support from our unit.

I had the privilege of being assigned CSSD-16's S-3 Training & Operations Non-Commissioned Officer (NCO) for our sixty - seventy-five-person unit depending on total manpower throughout the year.

During this tour, our combined unit's section teams upgraded major training components, ensured additional ground, infantry combat ready certifications, and increased total number of Marines fully qualified for duty and deployment.

One of the highlights in Yuma was designing, implementing, and managing the

Winter Field Operations for the (then) 385th Air National Guard's Black Hawk UH-60 Pilots stationed in Phoenix, Arizona.

Working closely with the 385th Senior Command, we ran their cold weather training qualifications during the bitter 1996 winter in Flagstaff for these pilots later deployed to the Balkans to support NATO operations. The winter was so cold that year our tanks containing the drinking water had be to warmed up as they had iced over inside!

Most of our CSSD-16 members trained alongside the black hawk pilots and crews "winter camping," receiving winter survival certifications, "breaking in" Mickey Mouse boots, winter tents, skis, snow shoes and cold weather specialty gear.

I finished my final year in Yuma, wrapping up nearly nine years in the Marine Corps as a senior Sergeant. I headed back to Michigan, in December 1997, to start an exciting ,new career in security and risk management support roles.

The Corps was now forever behind me, however the life lessons, relationships nurtured, and skills acquired will always be with me.

Honor. Courage. Commitment. Values worth living for. Values worth sacrificing for. Values that would sustain.

Chapter Seven

Civilian Again (1998 - 2012)

"They who can give up essential liberty to obtain a little temporary safety deserve neither liberty nor safety."
Benjamin Franklin (Memoirs)

Back in my beloved Michigan again! At my return, I immediately dived into the private sector risk management and security worlds which I had developed a passion for in the Marines serving around the globe.

I started out with a transportation security company, then transitioned to serving State Of Michigan senior enforcement directors, section heads, law enforcement leaders, and the Michigan State Police, Michigan Secretary of State, and select CEO's.

These challenging, senior assistant, government service opportunities prepared me to later work for a Michigan State Senator and Senate Majority Floor Leader as Office Manager, Executive Assistant, Assistant Constituent Aide, and Special Project Manager.

I worked sixty-hour weeks with the Senator's team and together we ensured his constituents received detailed and specialized care.

I closely coordinated with District officials, principals, and schools for the Senator's reading programs with young people, traveled to special events with military, legislative and other officials and served as primary gatekeeper to the Senator's office. No two days were the same!

I served under a veteran Chief of Staff who mentored, coached, and honed my civilian political skills to exacting, high standards. I owe much of my current success to this polished professional named Scott. Scott has been one of the best supervisors in my career.

Like SSgt Vanhorn, Scott was always there to support, whenever I needed anything to do my job better. Scott assigned challenging tasks, sometimes seemingly impossible, then cleared obstacles from my path, when necessary, to get those tasks done right.

After serving several years with my Senator, I received an unexpected call from the Office of The President for a former US

Attorney who had previously served a White House Attorney General. I remember that day! I nearly hung up the phone thinking the man on the other end was drunk, on drugs, or it was a prank call. It was no prank.

This global law firm had a need for an Office of The President Aide to fill a complex, dual professional role. This man had gotten my name (and resume) from Washington, D.C. where I had forwarded my resume thinking I might go back to D.C. to work. My resume had landed on this executive's desk strongly backed by a nationally legal friend who knew from me since being back in Michigan following Marine Corps service.

This complex, challenging role involved executive speech writing, correspondence for the President, Office of The President support, and designing a Risk Management Executive Administrator role for its senior team, Board of Directors, and one hundred law firm members.

I was flown to two states then interviewed by ten of its senior executives, Office of The President, and the President and his family members. It was made clear. No cobwebs would form under my feet. It would require eighty plus hour weeks to fulfill both roles.

The combined roles were required while this fast-growing firm positioned to expand to new global offices. Was I up for this tremendous challenge they wanted to know? After my due diligence, of course, I was up for the adventure! Back to the much warmer southwest I went.

During those fast-paced years, I helped this team setup global security operations, risk reduction policies, operational guidelines, templates, train the team, then travel across the nation in support of its Ambassador level events.

I had the privilege of managing our high risk, international security operations in London during its tragic bombings of July 2005.

While with the firm, I had the honor to work again with dozens of police agencies, executive protection professionals, state officials, U.S. Postal Service, U.S. Secret Service, other governmental and private agencies, U.S. Embassies, and foreign government and security management officials.

I maintain close relationships with those same executives and security professionals today.

Following this role, the next six years I worked in the private sector, where, combining with Greater Phoenix business owners, designed from scratch, a new, select client company (Scottsdale) during the second worst economic depression our County has ever faced.

Approximately five years later, I sold this company making the life defining decision to attend a ten-month police academy pursuing a dream germinating in my heart for the past two decades.

I was starting a new career in sworn law enforcement! However, it seemed I was simply coming home to my roots, to a close-knit family around whom I had served around the globe in special trust roles since 1989.

Chapter Eight

Police Academy Year (2012 - 2013)

"Courage is not the absence of fear, but rather the judgment that something else is more important than fear." Ambrose Redmoon

What drives human beings to pursue highly sacrificial professions? Doctors, nurses, teachers, police officers, fire fighters, military members – those who serve others on the "front lines" – what drives our desire to serve? We see both the best of society and the worst. Maybe the poem below says it best.

It was authored by retired Thibodaux, Louisiana Police Chief Scott Silverii, Ph.D.

The Final Inspection

The policeman stood and faced his God.
Which must always come to pass. He hoped his
shoes were shining just as brightly as his brass.
"Step forward now, policeman. How shall I deal
with you? Have you always turned the other
cheek? To My church have you been true?"

The policeman squared his shoulders and
said, "No, Lord, I guess I ain't. Because those
of us who carry badges can't always be a saint.

I've had to work most Sundays, and at times my talk was rough; and sometimes I've been violent, because the streets are awfully tough.

But I never took a penny that wasn't mine to keep......though I've worked a lot of overtime when the bills got just too steep. And I never passed a cry for help, though at times I shook with fear; and sometimes, God forgive me, I've wept unmanly tears.

I know I don't deserve a place among the people here. They never wanted me around except to calm their fear. If you've a place for me here, Lord, it needn't be so grand. I never expected or had too much, but if you don't...I'll

understand."

There was silence all around the throne
where the saints had often trod. As the
policeman waited quietly for the judgment of his
God. "Step forward now, policeman, you've
borne your burdens well. Come walk a beat on
Heaven's streets, you've done your time in hell."

This poem speaks to the heart of what every first responder has lived, breathed, and thought at times about life. First Responder work is a special calling, a noble career, however, tougher, more complex than ever before.

It requires an adversity tested Professional. An exceptionally mature, flexible, mentally tough, culturally sensitive, physically fit, courageous, diplomatic individual. You must be a high stakes, peace maker, orator, compassionate, a concise policy maker, excellent writer, public relations specialist, and independent thinker.

You must also be a seamless team player, self-motivated, knowing to your core you are called to do this tough work.

Police work requires uncommon courage, strong physical skills, tremendous endurance and the ability to face darkness yet never lose the truth that most humans are good, decent, and peaceful.

You must be mentally tough to remain healthy over a lifetime, yet emotionally courageous enough to process (all) the evil, sickness, suffering, violence, and tragedies you see every shift.

This can only be done through intentional functional fitness, non-law enforcement pursuits and endeavors, planned rest, great nutrition, and healthy supplementation when working the night shifts (Vitamin D, for example).

Even excellent policing changes you forever, however, you must decide how much. You must also have specific, healthy, pre- and post-shift routines that properly prepare you and then bring you back to real life after shift.

My Brothers and Sisters learning how to do these things (well), don't end up alcoholics, with trails of broken relationships, emotionally distant from loved ones, able to invest in others, and love serving society after retirement. It is not easy however it is possible.

I entered the academy at forty-seven years old.

Once again, I took on an impossible challenge some told me I would fail at. I embraced this challenge after seeking advice from my father in law (34 yrs. criminal justice service) and close friends having served decades in law enforcement.

When they confirmed (unanimously) that I had the life skills, maturity, and drive to accomplish this, I did not listen to the naysayers anymore. I am thankful I followed their expert advice!

I was affectionately nicknamed "Grandpa" and assigned command of my recruit class for all physical training, becoming its ceremonies drill master, managing inspections, formations, and events we participated in. It was a demanding role yet gave me the chance to again mentor younger professionals in my class.

My role empowered me (resources and authority) to encourage younger members facing subject matter challenges or fitness obstacle, to lead study sessions, and help fellow recruits maintain perspective during times when instructors pushed them beyond their known limits.

Class 74 was held at the new multi-million facility -- the Glendale Regional Public Safety Training Center (GRPSTC). We attended twelve to fifteen-hour days of demanding training, endless classes, off duty study sessions; defensive tactics, fire arms, high risk driving, and physical fitness five days a week while holding down full-time jobs in the civilian world.

Our days started before well before dawn ending long after the sun went down. We had no weekends – it was a sacrifice we were willing to make. A sacrifice we willingly made.

In addition, we were required to physically train on "days off" logging our training which was tested every weekend. You were all in or you could go home. A few went home because the demands were more than they were willing to pay.

To this day, I stay in close contact with my Command Staff from the leadership of Arizona Department of Public Safety (AZ DPS), Maricopa County Sheriff's Office (MCSO) and several other agencies leaderships comprising our Academy's Leadership and Core Instructor base.

They led us by example. They pushed us hard knowing law enforcement is not a profession for everyone. Better to learn that here then later on the street.

May 2013 came like a blur. Nearly 800 clock hours of actual classes, training, and class team projects were complete. Another 900 hours of class preparation and requirements around those 800 hours were now in the books.

Graduation was here! Could it be we had survived? The blood, sweat, and exhaustion of early morning dirt roads, training grinder, fire tower, and challenge runs. The days our bodies felt they would collapse (by 7 a.m.!) during Red Man fights, street survival scenarios, Police Officer Physical Ability Test (POPAT) challenge courses, and Cooper fitness tests – yet it was all worth it!

Agency Commanders from the Greater Phoenix Valley attended presenting our sworn officer badges that balmy May 2013 evening.

The relief, joy, and anticipation of working the street was just days away. It would be only days before we entered tough, Field Training Officer (FTO) training requirements every new officer must pass to exacting standards before going "solo."

I had the privilege to lead Class 74 through graduation ceremonies as Drill Leader, graduating with five others on the President's Academic List and as Distinguished Graduates for combined academic, leadership, proficiency and physical fitness excellence.

We voted "Tom" Class 74 Most Outstanding Graduate and Tom deserved it every step of the way! Before we were released by our Academy Commander, our Class shouted to our families and friends in the audience:

"Courage! Integrity! Sacrifice!" Little did I know Class 74's motto would become the critical traits required to survive, then overcome, severe tragedies pressed into my life from the outside in 2016 - 2018.

Chapter Nine

On the Street (2013 -)

Being a good police officer is one of the most difficult, dangerous, idealistic jobs in the world.
Thomas Hauser

Field Training Officer (FTO) required training lasts four months, sometimes longer. It is a rigorous, ten to fourteen hour shifts with seasoned street officers authorized to "sign off" on primary skills you must pass to go "solo." Only then, you go "solo" for a typical one-year probation.

During these probationary periods, you can be told to leave the blue line without cause.

I hit the beat in northern Arizona August 2013 with a fourteen-year street veteran, who pushed me harder than ever before. Big "Mac" was utterly professional, tough, yet incredibly funny.

Mac knew what it took to make it in the profession, to navigate its complexities, politics, having even been attacked and survived on the night streets. His manner was easy, self-assured, yet always ready for the unexpected. And did I mention he was funny? Mac could be pressing you hard one minute then busting your chops the next!

Only weeks into FTO leaving a juvenile scene, our pulses spiked as "that" hot tone (officer shot!) screeched out informing an AZ DPS (State Police) Brother had been shot south of town. Adam was a fourteen-year law enforcement veteran, a respected leader in our community. Adam's father had retired locally and Adam followed his father's footsteps serving with distinction with AZ DPS.

That night is crystal clear in my memory. A lifetime of emergency training, experience and crisis management immediately came back. The deranged killer was driving north bound, erratically, towards our current location fleeing units pursuing him.

We headed south, knowing Adam was probably bleeding out. No officer gets THAT text that you may face death's door that shift. We simply put on our ballistic vests every shift, stay strong, striving to make a difference just for one day.

We joined a rookie AZ DPS and our Sergeant in pursuit as I executed a reverse directional turn to pursue this deranged suspect.

Mac and I were now using breathing techniques to calm our physiology, minds and focus.

During crises, our bodies immediately turn on finely tuned survival systems. Fine motor skills decrease. Vision automatically narrows. Blood rushes to large muscle groups vs. small ones. This happens involuntarily. It is our fight or flight response.

These breathing techniques taught to special operations and first responder communities force our bodies back towards "normal" responses during high threat situations. We breathed prayers for Adam, that he was using these techniques too. He was. While bleeding out, Adam had returned to his patrol, radioed in the suspect's car description, then drove himself to our local ER.

Ten miles north during pursuit, we were ordered back to provide ER support for Adam's family and his blood covered team of doctors, nurses, working to save his life. I saw Adam for only seconds as doctors worked on him telling him I WOULD SEE him later.

Adam forced a smile (as only he could do!) telling me his mom was enroute—would I please met her outside and stay with her? I told him I had it covered – "just rest and let the Docs fix him up!"

I went out to find his mom arriving with his sister and other family members. This is a task no officer hopes to ever be assigned. To need to hold and attempt to comfort a Brother or Sister's family in crisis when outcomes are not known. Once she was safely with nursing staff, another officer stayed with her.

Big "Mac" then tasked me with chain of custody for Adam's marked patrol outside the ER. "No one is to touch anything inside the crime scene tape until Sheriff's Deputies arrive to relieve you."

Did I clearly understand and have any questions? As I said "yes" and then "no," I observed Adam's drying blood covering the entire outside of his front passenger door where he had leaned inside to radio he had been shot several times.

Behind his patrol were blood stained, transparent evidence bags full of Adam's uniforms, equipment and gear. It was sobering to stand there realizing Adam had slowed his breathing, literally saving his life, and driven himself to the ER. Otherwise, he would not be alive!

That event forever forged my officer safety awareness on hundreds of future traffic stops I made. On every call too. My nickname following FTO became "no hands Paulie" on the streets.

On every call, if my hands weren't in my pockets, yours weren't either. It was simply professionalism. A mutual courtesy extended to each other. No one ever got injured without the hands creating violence.

Within 30 minutes, the helipad was ablaze in light, its rotors talking, and Adam airlifted to a Phoenix trauma hospital for life saving care. Today, Adam is alive because gifted professionals worked hard to save him, and he had been trained to slow his breathing in severe crises.

During my remaining tour, I managed hundreds of felony cases, none of which went to trial. This was due to Big "Mac" and my veteran Sergeant (Les) demanding meticulous attention to detail every call or investigation from Day One. They pushed (in good ways) relentlessly making me a far better veteran officer. They deeply cared about our fellow citizens, their fellow officers, and me. It showed.

My other patrol cases ranged from stopping violent motorcycle gang fights, felony drug interdictions, aggravated DUI's, hundreds of traffic stops, HIDTA and SWAT support (high risk arrests), dozens of assaults, domestic violence, ID theft crimes, every crime type except murder and complex financial scheme crimes.

We had two major highways running through our jurisdiction. Both were drug "highways." "Finding" those drugs was a matter of being in the right place at the right time and ensuring no one's constitutional rights were ever violated.   Those rights we all treasure as "our" American rights. Unique rights given us by our Founding Fathers and state legislatures ever since.

My toughest cases were the suicides.

Each was sobering yet vastly different. It was critical to establish immediate rapport, genuine compassion, uniquely communicating with each grieving family member on scene.

In one case, with my Sergeant and fellow officers very close for safety, a distraught family member was "allowed" to beat the front of my ballistic vest, wailing in ways no human words can describe. That night, "comforting" WAS my assigned scene priority while fellow officers handled all other investigative roles with detectives.

Another overnight shift I remember like it was yesterday. Approximately 2:00 a.m. one Saturday, a hot tone screeched over our patrol radios. We had double squads (twice as many officers) and tonight that paid off. Dispatch indicated a domestic violence assault had occurred and the known, repeat offender, Thomas, was fleeing the scene after viciously attacking a former girlfriend.

Units responded, "Code 3" (lights and sirens) from everywhere. As I turned down a secondary street towards the reported scene, I visually identified Thomas, fleeing directly toward me in the roadway. I updated Dispatch and nearby officers attempted to locate him. Having "run Code 3," I immediately blocked off the road about fifty feet from Thomas. At gun point, I issued clear, verbal commands as fellow officers rushed to assist.

Thomas originally complied, however, smelled of alcohol, showing numerous physical signs he was probably on drugs, and as his hand cuffs were being placed, he broke free of restraint, physically attacking both me and another officer directly on my right side.

For those never experiencing the super human strength of a suspect high on multiple drugs (typically pain killing opiates) and alcohol they feel no pain. It may require several officers to simply bring them under control and then arrest such a suspect. Standing six feet two inches, two hundred thirty-five pounds and pumping iron regularly – to feel that super human strength from this kind of suspect (possibly 150 lb.) is something you never forget.

We fought hard defending ourselves from Thomas's assault for an exhausting (VERY long!) 30 seconds tumbling to the ground where we finally and safely restrained and cuffed him. Thomas was now screaming (as tape recorders ran) that he was "trying to kill" us. Recorders ran the next two hours, as Thomas told our Sergeant, fire paramedics, and ER staff "he had" decided to "commit suicide by cop" that night.

Later, paramedics and I transported Thomas to the ER for a documented, head to foot, detailed medical "clearance" before booking hours later. In jail terms, Thomas was a "straight back." Thomas was walked "directly back" to a special cell where he could not hurt himself (or fellow inmates) before seeing the Judge Monday in Court.

I went home that morning, tired, realizing (twice) I had been near death's door, and that professionalism, elite fitness, and officer teamwork had kept me alive another day.

I gave thanks for my Protection, dedicated fellow officers, and the privilege of being alive. Summer camp accident. College small town vehicle accident. Peruvian Pacific near drowning. Now my first "suicide by cop" attempt on my life. Life can be short. We never know. How we live matters.

In July 2015, I returned to the Phoenix Valley for unexpected reasons creating an AZ DPS licensed company. Ensured by Lloyd's of London, Eagle Int'l (EI) provided licensed and insured, special ops support, executive protection, special services, and risk and threat assessments to Fortune 100 companies.

I had the unique privilege to update former skills (for EI) with top Professionals across our nation. The next few years, these professionals were exceptionally gracious to me. They not only ensured prior risk and security management skills were refined back to a sharp edge, they mentored and spent personal time investing in me to ensure EI's success.

I honor you all here as I write. You remain the gold standard of our Profession: former POTUS detail members, US Secret Service Agents, national security, FBI, military, intelligence, retired law enforcement, and global specialty operators.

I remain indebted to you for your kindness, expertise and training. Many of you still work in the shadows. You prefer it that way. You do it for: Honor. Courage. Commitment. For our Country. Stay your course. Stay safe my Brothers and Sisters.

Over this time frame, EI then formed partnerships with globally respected companies, my former global network, working only with fully insured, state licensed companies. Together, combined response teams served a variety of high-risk situations, provided specialized assessments, managed a global company's Hurricane Harvey's Operations, served a complex government missing person case, and special units from US SOUTHCOM. We then managed a serious workplace violence matter for a global carrier working seamlessly with law enforcement, private security and ATAP Brothers and Sisters.

Chapter Ten

Overcoming Tragedy & Loss (2016 - 2018)

"One's best success comes after their greatest disappointments." Henry Ward Beecher

"Repetition does not transform a lie into a truth."
Franklin D. Roosevelt

"Is this all you want? You should pursue your gifts."
Jerry Hasenbein

Jerry Hasenbein.   This book is dedicated to Jerry and several others who deeply impacted my life.   Jerry was my father in law.

Jerry was diagnosed with dementia in 2011 which worsened until he crossed over in August 2018.

Jerry is the sole reason I had pursued a two decades old dream, beginning law enforcement service after working closely with Brothers and Sisters at the national and diplomatic levels since 1990.

Jerry had observed this undeveloped dream in my soul. He knew me inside and out from dozens of hours hiking the rugged trails of Greater Phoenix from 2006 - 2010.

Jerry closely observed my work ethic, integrity, character, training, and life experiences, then warmly, yet bluntly told me one day, it was a no brainer to pursue this life of service the rest of my life. It was up to me to pursue it all out.

Jerry had significantly invested in my Scottsdale company (twice) gaining a high return on investments in 2010 - 2011 before his tragic diagnosis, and then following my difficult choice to return to Phoenix July 2015, I had extended time with Jerry while running Eagle Int'l (EI).

I treasure these sacred times before Jerry passed. It was worth the tremendous career sacrifices to be at his side many times before he passed in August 2018. Those times live on in my memory as times of comforting him, singing to him, and saying goodbye over time to an outstanding Brother, Dear Friend and Confidant.

Jerry was a man of strong, simple faith. Though he could not speak now, he would smile as I read his favorite passages during our visits. After reading, I would hold his hand, and he would grip my hand powerfully each time! Towards the end of our times, he would always peacefully fall asleep as I said goodbye one more time.

When death comes knocking, as it will for us all, all seek something. I knew Jerry had made his peace long ago. We had talked often about all he had accomplished with his life. Jerry had achieved his top priorities, sacrificially loved his family, and in retirement, volunteered at the nature center and hospital to serve others.

Jerry was ready when the call came and I'm grateful his body no longer suffers with that brutal disease called dementia. Jerry finally received his promotion!

Except for those few years in Phoenix, I have passionately pursued this dream of service to my community and will for another two decades. I can't imagine doing anything else, remaining thankful for those who have given these new opportunities. I will pay your kindness forward as Jerry would have done to show his gratefulness.

I'm grateful I chose those short years away from law enforcement to say my final goodbyes to my Friend, Brother, and a Good Man. I will never regret it though a few did not understand and told me my sacrifices weren't worth it.

Jerry's character was unstoppable. His faithful belief in who I am changed my life for the decades to come. Because his influence was profound, I made the decision to live the remainder of my days in his honor. To practically (daily) live out the life priorities and character he modeled.

Jerry played a primary role in focusing my strengths as I learned about numerous "insurmountable" obstacles he had overcome.

Severe, tremendous adversities most never overcome.

Jerry grew up in a tough home life. He told me how he overcame things, so tough, they are not written down here. Jerry then went forward honorably serving thirty-four years in Wisconsin's criminal justice system.

From Jerry's influence, I now serve in a nationally respected youth mentorship program. I share how they too CAN journey with a few, well-chosen people to overcome their obstacles.

I am also the trained handler for a specialty dog, Zeus, who comforts terminally ill children. Jerry, I know you are smiling up there as I pay it forward. Semper FI Jerry!

During these (thankfully) same short years, I overcame severe tragedies and losses. Losses that could not be replaced. Losses that test you to the core.

I have always been type A. Always ready for any team challenge. I always live life to the fullest. I have always known the cup was half full. No matter the obstacles our team had to overcome. I remain a "positive pragmatist."

I have observed around our globe that the power of genuine love, human kindness, fitness, resiliency, unstoppable grit, and courageous perseverance is greater than any evil.

136

Whenever possible, we should stay clear of evil, however, sometimes it may come near our door. It must be directly faced, pushed away, in clear strength, courage, and through proactive action. To ignore it is to allow it to conquer our spirits, lives, and bring destruction to healthy living or to those we love.

I learned this at a far deeper level from 2016 - 2018. That uncommon courage, flexibility, discipline, perseverance, and resiliency are still daily choices. Individual choices every one of us must make especially in undeserved storms.

In reality, we control only a few things in life: 1. Our attitudes. 2. Our influence. 3. Our personal responsibility and effort levels. 4. How we respond to all of life.

We can choose to resent the undeserved, brutal storm; become angry, ugly and bitter, or learn to push forward, far deeper in character development becoming a better person in how we serve others both IN our storm and afterwards. Completely our choice.

No one can decide but each of us AND only we CAN decide to FACE the storm so it DEEPENS us.

I was also reminded that we CAN hold onto our core integrity through anything. No one can ever take that away from us. We have to give that up. Integrity is NOT about perfection, not making mistakes – we all blow it, make mistakes, etc.

It is owning our character, being the same person wherever you are – in public and in private – it is a JOURNEY.

And core integrity means that when we blow it, we make it right, we man up, we woman up, and genuinely apologize, when needed, and we learn from it. That is core integrity. It can never be taken away – only given away – or sold to the lowest bidder.

I have included several inspirational stories (Addendum III) for your consideration. These are real people who CHOSE to overcome overwhelming odds, terrible setbacks, and pursued integrity, hard work and service to others. All have made significant impacts with their lives. I pray they inspire you!

Like the above stories, when my unexpected, severe tragedies hit in 2016, they tested me to the core. I had not been irresponsible, made careless choices or brought any of these tragedies to my door. Sometimes life just happens as they say.

However, we are never victims. Refuse to ever be one in this life! That was a decision I also had to make.

Here's a final hard lesson I learned: We are all just one reality away from losses we didn't bring to ourselves.

A crippling accident. A life threatening or critical disease diagnosis. A career ending event. A paralysis. Loss of dear family. Loss of a spouse through death or otherwise.

We have no guarantees. So how we live our lives today matters. It matters that those we love and care for know it by our actions.

The point is NOT to fear what COULD happen, BUT to live NOW with thankfulness, diligence, and courage. To count our blessings every day. It means to tell those dear to you how special they are in creative meaningful ways.

When tragedy knocked in 2016, I remembered the summer ball bat near death experience. The Indiana car accident. The Peruvian Pacific near drowning, and other life and death events not shared in this book you now hold in your hands.

Will these tough challenges, I asked myself, even incredible tragedies make me better? I made my tough decisions to grow. Even more! That I would find new ways to serve.

I THEN surrounded myself with vetted, life tested warriors. Nationally respected men deeply tested, having tremendous mettle, those caring deeply for, and powerfully serving others through their lives. We locked arms then journeyed closely together and still do today.

143

Relationships forged in fire stand the test of time.

And together, WE resolved, no matter what, these storms would develop even stronger character, deeper hope, greater resiliency, and new compassionate services to others. They have and continue to do so.

I have not regretted that decision. I would make it again, one thousand times! I am stronger today for all that has been overcome these past two years. Jerry, you understand. You would have told me to do exactly what I did.

Tough yet tender. Courageous yet compassionate. Strong, yet always serving others at appropriate times. Showing respect to all, however, overcoming evil with GOOD.

Jerry, I know you are smiling. Rest in Peace Brother. We have the watch from here.

Another key survival pursuit was staying fit during the tests. Since 1990, I had pursued extreme and endurance sports, half marathons, Tough Mudders, etc.

I found in these a spiritual connection, a true compass, a clarity for life. Peak fitness had always empowered focused living, ensuring strong body, mind and soul for all challenges to come.

It was this same fitness, through these storms, my faith in God, other's strong faith in who I really am, and nationally respected mentors which TRULY sustained me as I created a new life in 2018 following these tragedies. I thank God for all these things!

Lastly, more than once, gracious, senior law enforcement Brothers (Sisters) journeyed with me as I created this new life. I journeyed with them too through the valley of death as we honored Tyler's and his family with the 100 Club of Arizona, AZ DPS, law enforcement, corrections, and dozens of officers from across Greater Phoenix. What an honor to serve in small ways caring for this dear family who suffered great loss! Rest in Peace Brother Tyler! You will NOT be forgotten.

Through these hardships, I have learned what REAL-LIFE IS. I am now a True Survivor. Not bitter. Better. Not angry. More courageous. Not fearful. More discerning.

True Survivors share a common language of compassion, courage, and clarity. I hope you will join me in becoming a True Survivor. Whatever your massive challenge is. We all have one sooner or later.

Since 1990, I was always assigned to build those unstoppable teams, overcome every challenge, conquer every task, crush every obstacle. NOW, I have been reminded how blessed we are to have wisely chosen those we closely journey with. It makes all the difference!

Many of you serve here in Arizona at senior levels of our best law enforcement agencies. Some of you serve nationally. Some in senior roles in D.C. Some in national roles in the Midwest.

You ALL remain people of deep character, uncommon integrity, and resiliency.

You have my respect for lives committed to character, excellence, integrity, and service to others! I honor you here, thanking you for all you have taught me these most recent years. First, by personal example, then through your character, standing firmly alongside me as I re-enter further sworn service to my community.

Semper Fidelis (Always Faithful!)

Addendum I: Notes About Author

Paul is a Spanish street speaker, loves all things southwest, settling here after serving around the globe with senior government, military, and in the global security and risk management sector.

Paul's been rigorously subjected to over one dozen lifetime background investigations, and numerous polygraphs for top clearances and special trust roles assigned by the government, military and law enforcement (1990 – 2017). Paul likes to joke that even the color of his socks must be noted "somewhere!" He is thankful to all who gave him a chance!

However, Paul's professional background does not define him. He says he is "an ordinary man simply provided extraordinary opportunities and these team successes are <u>not</u> his greatest accomplishments."

Paul's greatest success was finding rigorously selected professionals to whom he first humbles himself, then carefully listens to, seeks counsel from, and then closely journeys with to make the big decisions of life. His core values

remain: Honor. Clarity. Courage. Integrity.
Sacrifice.

A decorated Marine Sergeant (Middle East
& Other Theaters) Paul learned from his earliest
days a man only becomes as solid as those he
surrounds himself with. Paul is blessed to have
key professionals speaking into his life today so
he stays his course.

Paul and "Z" will continue comforting
tragedy impacted and terminally ill children (Paul
is trained handler for Zeus a specialty therapy dog
for kids). He will be presenting to classrooms,

special events, and to at risk youth on behalf of the Travis Manion Foundation next year.

A street tested, discerning officer, Paul remains committed to this complex role and will continue serving and protecting with excellence.

Paul remains an avid endurance athlete, loves the outdoors, a great cup of coffee, his family and vetted law enforcement Brothers and Sisters. Paul is committed to honoring the legacy left by his close friend Jerry Hasenbein and his Brother "Rudy." Rest in Peace, Jerry and Rudy, WE have the watch from here.

Paul and "Zane" – Northern Arizona Pals!

Adopted Brother Rudy (EOW: March 2017

VFW, Vice Commander, Marine, Desert Storm

Veteran

Rest in Peace Brother I Will Help Care For Your

Family

"Z" Finally Graduates: Comforts

Terminally Ill Youth

Remembering Our Fallen

AZ DPS Brother Tyler!

Working Hurricane Harvey: Emergency

Operations For Global Company

Challenge Coins From Close Friend

8th & I Barracks, Washington, D.C.

Guest of USMC Commandant

Meeting General (Stormin' Norman)

Schwarzkopf (Cairo)

UNITED STATES MARINE CORPS
MARINE SECURITY GUARD BATTALION
2037 ELLIOT ROAD
QUANTICO, VIRGINIA 22134-5025

IN REPLY REFER TO
1650
MSGBn
1 Jul 93

From: Commanding Officer
To: Whom it may concern

Subj: LETTER OF RECOMMENDATION

1. Sergeant Paul A. Snyder served in a most demanding assignment as a Marine Security Guard. He was first selected from a large number of Marine Corps volunteers and then subjected to a very rigorous screening and training process. During this training, attrition was extremely high because of the standards required at foreign service posts where Marines receive a Security Clearance. Operational duties were performed under instructions dictated by the Department of State, Ambassadors, and Consul Generals. The constant daily demand for integrity, loyalty, initiative, and personal appearance were far beyond those of an average Marine Sergeant.

2. Sergeant Snyder served with distinction as a Marine Security Guard in Cairo, Egypt from November 1990 to March 1992; Lima, Peru from March 1992 to June 1993. As his Commanding Officer I can positively state that I would trust him completely in any assignment. He is totally dependable and will perform superbly under extreme pressure. I would eagerly seek Sergeant Snyder's services where the highest moral and personal character is required.

J. R. BENSON
Colonel, U. S. Marine Corps
Commanding

MSG Battalion Commander's Letter

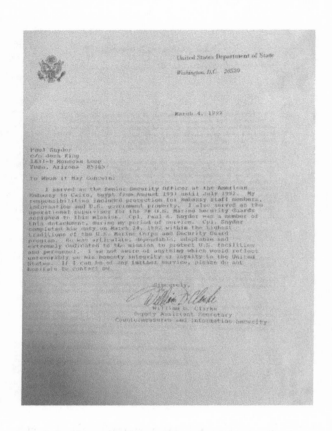

Ambassador Clarke's Letter

Certificate of Achievement

Presented to

Paul Andrew Snyder

{Graduated with Distinction}

In recognition of successful completion of the 585-hour Basic Peace Officer Course Approved by the Arizona Peace Officer Standards and Training Board and prescribed by Arizona Administrative Code R13-4-110.

Glendale Community College Law Enforcement Training Academy
Name of Academy

May 17, 2013
Date of Graduation

Academy Commander/Director

Lyle W. Mann, AZ POST, Executive Director

Law Enforcement

Academy Graduation!

Business Trip (Washington, D.C.)

Working The Streets

Of Northern Arizona

Tough Mudder 2015 (AZ)"Another Day In
Paradise:" A 11.3 Mile Obstacle Course

Addendum III: Overcomer Stories*

https://www.amazon.com/Rowdy-Rising-Unrivaled-Dainon-Moody/dp/1943307040
(Rudy Gaines Story)

https://www.amazon.com/gp/product/0439131952/ref=dbs_a_def_rwt_bibl_vppi_i0
(Mae Jemison Story)

https://www.amazon.com/dp/098865198X/ref=rdr_ext_sb_ti_hist_1
(Karen Perry Story)

https://www.amazon.com/Burning-Shield-Jason-Schechterle-Story/dp/0988651947/ref=sr_1_1?ie=UTF8&qid=1549121637&sr=8-1&keywords=burning+shield
(Jason Schechterle Story)

https://vimeo.com/18786500
https://www.amazon.com/Long-Run-Firefighters-Triumphant-Comeback/dp/1609611799
(Matt Long Story)

The above hyperlinks are provided solely for personal educational use only. Author, in no way, assumes any legal responsibility, or any liability for, concerning, in connection to, or with, support between, from, or with Amazon and Vimeo, authors or individuals above whatsoever. These hyperlinks are provided solely as motivational information always available 24/7 on the internet to anyone. Reader assumes all responsibility, liability, for use, reliance upon, or in utilizing all above links, strictly a personal decision to view from internet and available 24/7.

Paul is a spanish street speaker, loves all things southwest, settling here after serving around the globe with senior government, military, and in the global security and risk management sector. Paul's been rigorously subjected to over one dozen lifetime background investigations, and numerous polygraphs for top clearances and special trust roles assigned by the government, military and law enforcement (1990 – 2017). Paul likes to joke that even the color of his socks must be noted "somewhere!" He is thankful to all who gave him a chance!

Copyrighted Photo 2019

Made in USA - Kendallville, IN
1067843_9781796298369
04.02.2020 1145